HAGGADAH
OF
POEMS
FOR THE
PASSOVER
SEDER

POEMS BY
SUSAN DUBIN
2018

**ISBN-13:
978-1986356848**

**ISBN-10:
1986356841**

INTRODUCTION

The holiday of Passover is the cornerstone of the Jewish religion. The Jews became a nation with the exodus from Egypt and the acceptance of the Torah, God's law. The exodus is remembered in almost every prayer recited in Jewish worship.

Moreover, the escape from slavery, the parting of the Red Sea, and the journey through the desert to Sinai and the land of Israel has captured the imagination of the people of the world. Indeed, Christians and Muslims look to Moses as a key figure in determining their history. In Christianity, Jesus's last supper was, in fact, the Passover seder.

There are hundreds of versions of the Haggadah, the retelling of the story of the exodus and the blueprint for how to conduct a seder. This is my version. I use the traditional format, but I coach each ritual in a poem.

The commandment was to tell the story to each generation. Hopefully my retelling will help new generations remember and tell the story to their children.

ORDER OF THE SERVICE

Leader:

All: Freedom must come from order.
Order in our lives gives us freedom to explore.
Order to our thoughts leaves room for imagination.
Order in our telling gives meaning to our story.

Leader: This is the order of our seder:

Participant: First we bless the candles

Participant: Then we bless the wine.

All: A holy space is thereby marked in our mundane world.

4

Participant:	We are commanded to welcome and to serve the needy.
	Now we welcome the stranger.
All:	Let all who are hungry, come and eat.
Participant:	Wash hands.
All:	Prepare a clean space for freed hearts.
Participant:	Dip the greens in salty tears.
	The symbol of spring replaces the winter of weeping.
All:	Renewal of hope in the pool of misery.
Participant:	Next we break the middle matzah.
	The bread of affliction,
	Symbol of our haste,
	Is broken in its heart.
All:	The hidden piece allows us to hold back
	Let our hurry wait.
Participant:	After dinner, after the story is told,
All:	We will search for the Afikomen,
	the HIDDEN PIECE,
	The piece we need to be whole.
Participant:	And why?
	Why do we celebrate?
	Why do we eat like this?
	Why?
All:	Ask and answer.

Participant: Ah, the story...

Participant: Let me tell you...
               If you only knew...
               You wouldn't believe it...
All: But, it's true!

Participant: The ten plagues recounted
All: Dayenu
               Enough

Participant: A second cup of wine

All: Halleluyah, we praise G-d.

Participant: Matzah to eat
All: (To eat, at last!)

Participant: Matzah alone,
               Matzah and bitter herbs,
               Matzah and sweet charoset dipped in bitter
               herbs.

Participant: Charoset and Matzah.
               And Charoset.
               More Charoset.
All: Never enough sweetness to replace bitter
               memory.

Participant: Dinner, too?
All: Dayenu!
               Enough food.
               Dayenu!

Participant: Find the afikomen.

Participant: Now blessings.

Participant: We welcome Elijah
Not stranger but guide.

All: We are free,
But we are promised more than mere
freedom.
Bring us Shalom, the wholeness of peace.

Participant: Two more cups of wine.
Next year together again in health, we pray.

All: Sing then of our journey
From bondage to freedom
From narrow thoughts to open acceptance
From sorrow to joy.
Thank G-d for our seder
Thank G-d for our freedom
Thank G-d for our lives.

Leader: # THE SEDER PLATE

The plate tells the story through
Smell
And
Taste
And
Sight
And
Memory.

Participant: The roasted egg, **B'ETZAH**, reminds us of the
sacrifice at the Temple, long since destroyed.
It reminds us of our pagan roots,
A people who did not lose touch
with its promise of fertility.

Participant: The **KARPAS**, dark green parsley,
light green celery,
Sings of Spring
And growth and
New beginnings.

Participant: The **Z'ROAH**, roasted bone,
Another symbol of sacrifice,
But this, a darker one.
Blood on the doorposts,
Reminds us
Freedom comes with a price.

Participant: **MAROR**, Bitter herb,
Bitter taste,
Bitter people who must dwell as slaves.
Smelling the horseradish root as it is ground,
Brings the tears
That cleanse our eyes
And our memories.

Participant: Sweet **CHAROSET**,
Apples and Honey, Raisins and Dates,
Nuts and Fruit and Wine.
Looking like the mortar that held the bricks,
But the sweetness belies the terror.
The taste reminds us how delicious is
Freedom,
How sweet it is to escape.

BLESSINGS #1
CANDLES AND SHECHEHEYANU

CANDLES

Participant: We light these candles as commanded.
We light these candles to mark our home as a holy place.
We light these candles to illuminate our hearts
as we turn to G-d.

All: Baruch atah adonai elohenu melech haolam
asher kid'shanu b'mitzvotav v'tzivanu l'hadlik ner shel
(Shabbat v') Yom Tov.

SHECHEHEYANU

All: To be here,
With you,
In health,
Is answered prayer.

Baruch atah adonai elohenu melech haolam
shecheheyanu, v'keyamanu, v'higigeyanu lazman hazeh.

BLESSINGS #2
KIDDUSH

BLESS THE WINE

All:
Holy is joy.
Sanctified is happiness.
Praise G-d for wine.

Baruch atah adonai elohenu melech haolam, boreh pree ha gafen.

Drink the first cup of wine

11

WELCOMING THE NEEDY

Participant:	Open the door to welcome the stranger.
Participant:	Open the door to all in need.
Participant:	Share your bounty with any who want.
Participant:	Share your dinner with any in despair.

All:	Remember the downtrodden
	Because you once walked there.

Break the middle matzah to hide for the afikomen.

BLESSINGS #3

KARPAS
GREEN VEGETABLE

All: Blessed is G-d who makes
green things grow from
the earth.

Baruch atah adonai elohenu melech haolam boreh pree haadomah.

Dip the green vegetable into salt water and eat it.

13

Leader: ## THE FOUR QUESTIONS MORE OR LESS

All: Why?

Participant:
Please tell me
I want to know
How is tonight different?

Participant:
Yes, we eat the bitter herbs.
True, we eat unleavened bread.
Of course, we dip our celery and our horseradish.
Pillows help us lean as we eat like Roman Senators.

All: But why?

Participant:
Is it only tradition?
A commandment of G-d?

Participant: Do we remember the taskmasters?
Participant: Do we remember the Pharaoh?
Participant: Do we remember our tears?
Participant: Do we remember the exodus?

All:
What is the way to understand all this?
Or is it only important that we keep asking

WHY?

B'SEDER

Participant:
Everything's in order
Kol b'seder.
The cleaning
The shopping
The cooking
Table is set with china and silver and linen and flowers and piled high with food.

All:
Is this how we remember slavery?
A contrast to abundance?

Participant:
Is not this most important holiday,
The centerpiece of our faith,
The definition of who we are as a people,
More than cooking and cleaning and food?

Participant:
Have the symbols become the reality?

All:
Kol b'seder?
Are we really okay?

THE STORY

Leader: And the children of Jacob, also known as Israel
went down to Egypt
Because there was a great famine in the land.
Joseph, Jacob's favorite son, welcomed them in the
name of the Pharaoh.
There they lived in the land of Goshen
for four hundred years.
But a new king who did not know Joseph became Pharaoh.
He saw the prosperity of the Israelites
and was afraid.

Participant: "In time of war, they may join an enemy
Against me," he said.
"They must be destroyed."

Leader: So, he issued a decree that all male children
Born to the Israelites
Be thrown into the Nile.

16

Furthermore, he enslaved the people
and forced them to make bricks
and build the cities of Pithom and Ramses.

All: The people cried out to G-D to save them.

Participant: Did G-d not promise their ancestor Abraham
that they would be as numerous as the stars?

Participant: Did G-d not promise Isaac
that his children would prosper?

Participant: Did Jacob not teach
that G-d would redeem them?

Participant: Where was this G-d?

Leader:	It was Moses, the child rescued from the Nile Raised by the Egyptian princess, who gave the answer.
Participant:	In a desert hideaway, he heard the voice of G-d speak to him from a burning bush.
Participant:	"Come unto Egypt and tell Pharaoh to let my people go!"
All:	And Moses did as G-d commanded.

FOUR WISE WOMEN TELL THE TALE

Read responsively:
No wise, no wicked, no simple, no young.
In my mother's house there were two daughters,
not four sons.
But the story was told the same.
Where were the mothers?
I wanted to know.
Where were the daughters of the Exodus?

Enough of Pharaoh and Aaron and Jethro and even Moses.
Tell me of the women.

If not for the women, we would be slaves.
The midwives are the true heroes of this story.
G-d did nothing when Pharaoh decreed
All male children should be thrown in the Nile.

Amram merely wept and avoided his wife.
But the midwives defied their king.
They birthed a people.

Now let me hear the story of the women.
Their voice too long silent as we learn the
Song of freedom, The means of deliverance,
The passage through the waters of life.

All: Thank G-d for the women who make us free.

19

KOL ISHA

All: Too long have we been silent.
Our voices long ignored.
Too long have we been silent.
Our stories must be heard.
Listen to our anger.
Recognize our pain.
Too long have we been silenced.
It's time to know our names.

Participant: We are the mothers of the Exodus.
Participant: Yochevet,
Participant: Batyah,
Participant: Miriam,
Participant: Zipporah.

All: We are the women who eased
the passage of our people
out of Mitzrayim.
Moses, G-d's beloved, was
our son,
our brother,
our love.
The Almighty spoke to him face-to-face.
Yet we were the ones who

Participant:	Nurtured him,
Participant:	Taught him,
Participant:	Prepared him,
Participant:	Loved him.

Participant:

I, Yochevet, gave him life
and set him afloat on the Nile.
I suckled him when he was drawn from the river.

Participant:

I, Batyah, found him in his basket
and raised him as an Egyptian prince.
When he brought his people out of Egypt,
I gave up my homeland and went with him.

Participant:

And I, Miriam, watched over him as sister
and helped him lead our people as prophetess.
The women turned to me at the Red Sea
To lead their celebration of freedom.

Participant:

I, Zipporah, sheltered him in the wilderness
When he fled the wrath of Pharaoh.
He chose me,
His dark desert princess,
To bear his sons.
It was my knife that circumcised our child
and brought him to G-d.

All:

We are the women of Moses,
The beloved of G-d.

Yes, listen to our stories.
Understand our pain.
Too long have we been silent.
It's time all know our names.

Participant:

YOCHEVET :
MOSES'S MOTHER

I am his mother.
A slave.
A Hebrew.
He has been hidden these weeks since his birth.
This child that almost didn't come to be.
And now
What am I to do?
I can no longer hide him.
His cries will condemn us all to death.
But I am his mother.
How can I set him afloat on the Nile?
This basket, so thin,
Protect my child.
Rock him to sleep.
Keep him safe.
Set him free.

Participant:

BAT-YA:
THE EGYPTIAN PRINCESS WHO RAISED MOSES

I know loneliness.
I, Bat-Ya, Daughter to a god who ruled Two Kingdoms,
I, Bat-Ya, Pharaoh's daughter, yet never to be queen.
I, Bat-Ya, Pharaoh's sister, but never to be wife.
I, Bat-Ya, loved by all,
But never beloved by my own belov'ed.

Once I was Mother to a child not my own,
But now he has gone to find his G-d.
He searches for peace within himself.
He yearns to set his people free.

Once I was at home among my people,
But now I am a stranger in my own land.
Where will I find peace? Who will set me free?

I know loneliness.
I wander with the people of my son.
I search for freedom with their G-d.
I, Bat-Ya, daughter of the Nile,
I, Bat-Ya, daughter of G-d.
I, Bat-Ya, beloved of the One who rules the world.

Participant:

MIRIAM'S PLEA:
A SISTER'S WORDS

I am Miriam.
Yohevet's only daughter.
Amram's outspoken child.
Aaron's jealous sister.
Moshe's watchful guardian.

I am Miriam.
Miriam of the Red Sea's song.
Miriam of the dance by the Sea of Reeds.
Miriam, the voice in the desert that will not be silenced.

I am Miriam.
Miriam of bitter loneliness.
Miriam of wild rejoicing.
Miriam, the keeper of sweet waters.

Pass the Cup of Miriam around and have each person pour a little of the water into their own clear glass .
Drink the water after reciting:

Baruch atah adonai eloheynu melech ha-olam, borey et ha-mayim.

Cut the orange and each eats a slice after saying:
Baruch atah adonai eloheynu melech ha-olam, borey pree ha-etz.

All: I am Miriam.
I dance for the tribe of Dinah.
I sing for the children of Israel.
I am Miriam.
Remember me.

25

ZIPPORAH :
MOSES'S WIFE

Zipporah, desert princess,
Linked forever to my shepherd prophet,
Consort to G-d's chosen,
Stranger to his people,
Yet mother of blessings.

May I be like Sarah and Rachel.
Not the dark sister,
But a bringer of light.

I am not a singer like sister Miriam.
Nor can I dance.
But sacrifice I know,
And loneliness.

Not for me the timbrel and the lyre.
Not for me rejoicing on the shore.
I hold the bloodied knife
And remind my lord of his duty and his promise.

I am Zipporah, Daughter of Jethro,
Mother of Gershom, bridegroom of blood,
Wife of Moses.
I am the stranger in your midst.
Welcome me.

THE TEN PLAGUES

As the plagues are recited, pour a drop of wine out of your cup for each plague. Recite together:

BLOOD fills the waters.   ***Daum***

FROGS hop on Pharaoh's face.   ***Tzfardea***

LICE itch and bite and scrabble everywhere.   ***Kinim***

WILD BEASTS appear to ravage flocks.   ***Arov***

MURRAIN kills cattle left and right.   ***Dever***

BOILS break out on face and hands.   ***Shchin***

HAIL of ice burns the land.   ***Barad***

LOCUSTS swarm through field and house.   ***Arbe***

DARKNESS covers all with fear.   ***Choshech***

SLAYING OF THE FIRST BORN   ***Makat Bechorot***

Dayenu.   Enough.   Dayenu.

Go free.
But at what price?

BLESS THE WINE

All:
We drink to remember.
We drink to forget.
**Baruch atah adonai elohenu melech haolam
boreh pree ha gafen.**
Drink the second cup of wine

BLESSINGS #4
WASHING HANDS

Leader:

Yes, there is a prayer for everything.
Cleanliness is godliness.
Praise G-d for commanding our health.

All: **Baruch atah adonai elohenu melech haolam asher
kidshenu b'mitzvotav al nitiliyat yadiiyim.**
Wash hands in preparation for the meal.

BLESSINGS#5
MATZAH

Participant : **EATING MATZAH**
Even though we can't eat bread
The blessing that we said
Thanks G-d for bread.
It's flat.
That's that.

All: Baruch atah adonai elohenu melech haolam
hamotzee lechem min haaretz.
Baruch atah adonai elohenu melech haolam
asher kidshenu b'mitzvotav
al acheelat matzah.
Eat the Matzah.

BLESSINGS#6
MAROR

Participant: ## EATING BITTER HERBS
Sharp taste brings tears to dry eyes
Reminding us of bitter thoughts and sharp memories
And tears yet to shed.

All: **Baruch atah adonai elohenu melech haolam
asher kidshenu b'mitzvotav
al acheelat maror.**

*Eat the bitter herbs on Matzah.
Then make a sandwich of bitter herbs and Charoset and eat it.*

DINNER

Find and share the
afikomen for dessert.

BLESSINGS#7

Thank You, LORD!

AFTER THE MEAL

All: Thank you for the food
That filled our mouths and nourished our bodies.
Thank you for the conversation that opened our minds
And nourished our intellect.
Thank you for the love of family and friends that crowded
out our loneliness
And nourished our hearts.

ELIJAH

Open the door and sing "Eliyahu HaNavi, Eliyahu Ha tishbe, Eliyahu, Eliyahu, Eliyahu Hagiladi."

All:

Pour your wine into the Cup.
It is for Elijah.
Share the burden.
Help him to bring an era of
PEACE for all.
Help him to bring an end to want.
Help us to bring SHALOM.

Everyone pours a little of their wine into Elijah's cup. The cup is then passed around and all take a sip. Sing "Osay shalom bimromav, hu ya'aseh shalom aleinu, v'imru, imru amen"

BLESSINGS#8

BLESS THE WINE

Participant: To a world that is whole,
One in peace.

All: **Baruch atah adonai elohenu melech haolam
Boreh pree ha gafen.**

Drink the third cup of wine

BLESSINGS#9

BLESS THE WINE

Participant: Our seder's almost finished.
Next year...
Again in peace.

All: **Baruch atah adonai elohenu melech haolam
boreh, pree ha gafen.**

Drink the fourth cup of wine

FROM NARROW PLACES

Read verses responsively:

And you shall tell your children on that day,
"It is because we were slaves,
And now we are free."

Each of us faces the coming forth.
Each of us leaves our Mitzrayim.
Narrow places define our struggle.
The slavery of
Narrow thoughts
And deeds undone
Come forth as
The blossoming of a soul
That stretches
To understand the world.

All: It is because we were slaves
That now we can be free.

Made in United States
Orlando, FL
30 March 2024

45291084R00020